Dresden

Illustrated guide to the state capital and surrounding area

Famous view of Dresden from the right bank of the Elbe underneath Augustus Bridge, engraving by Canaletto (1721–1780)

Text: Wolfgang Kootz · Photos: Dietmar Berthold

B&V Verlag, Dresden

The history of Dresden

927–29	Colonisation of the Slavs east of the Elbe by King Henry I, Duke of Saxony, who also built a castle in Meissen.
10th C.	Margravate of Meissen becomes the heartland of the later Electorate of Saxony.
1089	The House of Wettin is given the margravate as a fief.
ca. 1200	A margraval castle is built in "Drezdzany".
1206	"Dresdene" mentioned in records.
1216	"Neuendresden" is indicated as a town on the right bank of the Elbe opposite the village of "Altendresden".
ca. 1300	Construction of a castle and town fortifications.
1403	Altendresden receives town charter.
1423	King Sigismund grants the Duchy of Saxe-Wittemberg to Frederick the Warlike as a fief together with the title of elector. The entire territory is soon known as Saxony or Electoral Saxony. The Wettin family has the Albrechtsburg built in Meissen to replace the Romanesque castle.
1464	Following the death of Frederick the Gentle his sons Earnest and Albert reign together. They select Dresden as their seat.
1485	Treaty of Leipzig: the territory is divided up between Earnest and Albert. Dresden becomes the seat of the Albertine succession.
1491	Following a devastating fire, the town is rebuilt with stone houses and tile roofs.
ca. 1500	The castle in the old town is converted into a palace and the old town walls fortified. Remnants facing the Elbe can still be seen today.
1517	Martin Luther preaches in the palace chapel.
1539	Reformation in Dresden.
1547	Duke Maurice becomes prince elector. The palace is enlarged.
1685	Fire in Altendresden. A "new town" (Neustadt) is built in which stone houses are compulsory.
1694	Frederick Augustus I, known as Augustus the Strong, becomes prince elector.
1697	Augustus the Strong and the entire court convert to Catholicism. He becomes King of Poland and ruler of one of the largest territories in Europe. On the model of King Louis XIV of France he embarks on an extravagant building spree. Works of world renown are erected in Dresden and surrounding area: the Zwinger (from 1710), the Court Church (Hofkirche) and the castles of Moritzburg and Pillnitz. Augustus gathers an impressive collection of objets d'art.

Frederick Augustus I (the Strong) Elector of Saxony and King of Poland, 1670 – 1733

1708	The alchemist Böttger invents European porcelain in Dresden.
1710	Founding of the first European porcelain factory in the Albrechtsburg in Meissen.
1719	Magnificent ceremony to mark the marriage of Elector Frederick August to the Maria Josepha, daughter of the Habsburg emperor.
1733	Death of Augustus the Strong. His son, Frederick Augustus II, also King of Poland (Augustus III) continues the extravagant collections. A gilded equestrian statue in Neustadt marketplace is erected in memory of his illustrious father.
1756 – 63	The splendour of the royal seat is tarnished as a result of the Seven Years' War. Many buildings are destroyed and Saxony is called upon to pay considerable reparations.
1806	Saxony joins Napoleon's Confederation of the Rhine and becomes a kingdom.
1809	Napoleon has the fortifications dismantled.
1815	Congress of Vienna: Saxony loses half of its territory to Prussia.
1839	Opening of Germany's longest railway of the time from Dresden to Leipzig.
1849	May insurrection in Dresden put down by the army.
1918	Abolition of the monarchy. Dresden becomes capital of the Free State of Saxony.
1945	Massive air raids by English and American bombers destroy the city centre on 13/14 February, killing around 25,000 people.
1952	Dissolution of the Länder (states) in the former East Germany. Dresden becomes one of fourteen regional capitals.
1990	With the reunification of Germany Dresden becomes capital of the Free State of Saxony.
2006	The Palace and the Church of Our Lady are reconstructed in time for Dresden's 800th anniversary.
2012	The garden city of Desden Hellerau applies to become a World Heritage Site.

A tour of Altstadt (West Bank)

Elbe silhouette

Like the mythological phoenix rising from the ashes, Dresden has re-established its excellent reputation as a cultural centre following the devastating fire bombing of 13 February 1945. To obtain a first impression of the charm of this city it is best viewed from across the Elbe near the Augustus Bridge (**Augustusbrücke**) ①. Here the city's distinctive panorama, famous for centuries and a continuing attraction for painters from all over Europe, can be admired: in the foreground the banks of the Elbe and the river itself with the delightful bridge, and in the background an array of impressive buildings with the George Gate (Georgentor) of the royal palace in the centre, to the left the massive, dark Ständehaus, the friendly Sekundogenitur with its enchanting spire, the long facade of the Art Academy with its round dome, the massive Albertinum, and finally Brühl Terrace, the "balcony of Europe" in front. This is now overlooked by the dome of the Church of Our Lady. To the right of the bridge are the Cathe-

dral (katholische Hofkirche) and the celebrated Semper opera house, with the intricate Italian Village (Italienisches Dörfchen) in front of the world famous Zwinger. To the right of the Opera House is the new Landtag (state parliament) with its glass front, designed by Peter Kulka and completed in 1994. This is followed by the extensive New Congress Centre to the west. The imposing Erlweinspeicher, which was once a warehouse but today a hotel, is situated behind it. At the end of St Mary's Bridge (Marien-brücke) the mosque-like Yenidze, a former cigarette factory designed by M. Hammitzsch, rounds off the ensemble.

As far back as the 13th century a stone bridge spanned the river between the two settlements. The bridge was altered by Pöppelmann in 1727–31 during the reign of Augustus the Strong to form a linking element incorporating the river itself. To meet the needs of modern traffic it was rebuilt in 1907–10 by Kreis and Klette. By using Pöppelmann's original concept they were able to ensure that the outward appearance of the bridge remained intact.

View from the Carola Bridge (Carolabrücke) of the Brühlsche Terrasse with Hausmann Tower, the Ständehaus (ex-Parliament), the Hofkirche and the Semper Opera House

Royal Palace ② (Residenzschloss)

From Augustus Bridge the visitor goes straight across the Schlossplatz to the Georgenbau at the entrance to the castle, built in 1530 in a late Renaissance style as a residence of Duke George the Bearded. In spite of renovations in 1969 the building is almost black as a result of the high iron content in Saxon sandstone, not to mention the influences of the weather and exhaust

Courtyard of the Royal Palace – restored facade with its fabulous decorative elements

Detail of the west wing of the castle

View of the west wing of the castle from Theaterplatz (Theatre Square)

fumes. The Georgenbau forms the link between the stables to the left and the palace buildings which were erected from 1500 onwards to replace the castle on the Taschenberg. In 2006 the palaces around the Hausmann Tower returned to their former regal splendour, taking visitors back to the days when the palace formed the heart of this powerful territory. Also the famous art collections are back to their original location: the Copper Etching Cabinet, the Coin Cabinet, the Art Library, the Armoury and, above all, the legendary **Treasure Chamber** of Augustus the Strong will be situated in the palace's recreated **"Green Vaults"**. In its thirty years at the Albertinum, the latter collection attracted around 19.5 million visitors.

The treasury in the green-painted vault of the Royal Palace already had its admirers back in 1680. But it was only thanks to the extravagant collecting tastes of Augustus the Strong and his son Augustus III that it developed into what it is today, namely the most important collection of its type in Europe. Visitors viewing these precious and masterfully worked materials could think themselves in Ali Baba's Cave. The exhibition is housed in the amber cabinet and in the seven rooms of the historic treasury. Of particular merit are the artistic works of court jeweller Dinglinger who made the "Golden Coffee Service" for Augustus the Strong with

Georgenbau, Renaissance palace up to Brühl Terrace

with magnificent portals and gabled buildings, seen from steps leading

its enamelled cups richly ornamented with precious stones, and what is possibly the most popular exhibit, the famous Court of Delhi on the Birthday of the Grand Mogul with its 137 golden, colourfully enamelled figures decorated with over 5,000 diamonds, rubies, emeralds and pearls. It cost the rulers almost 60,000 talers, much more than the shell of the elaborate Moritzburg hunting lodge. Even more valuable from an artistic point of view is Dinglinger's Diana Bathing, his favourite work, depicting the mythological scene in which the unapproachable goddess Diana changes a youth into a stag and has him torn to pieces by dogs for having watched her bathing. The value of many apparently insignificant works only becomes evident on closer inspection – like the cherry stone which, when seen under a magnifying glass, reveals carved human heads. More conspicuous is the 16th and 17th century jewellery with nine complete

◀ *Details: the dromedary*

"Delhi Court"

▼ *The white elephant*

◀ *The hunting elephant*

"Delhi Court": details

Palace:
Green Vaults, Copper Etching Cabinet, Armoury,
Turkish Chamber, Coin Cabinet: *Wed.–Mon. 10 am – 6 pm.*
Visitor's service: Tel. 0391 49142000, www.skd.museum

Green Vaults: Golden coffee set by Dinglinger

14

sets of matching jewels which go to make up the largest historical jewellery treasure in Europe. With all this magnificence on show, it should not be forgotten that because of space constraints only about half of the exhibits can be seen. The entire collection with about 3000 exhibits, after moving from the Albertinum, came back to its original location in 2006.

The **Copper Etching Cabinet** (Kupferstichkabinett) and Coin Cabinet is now also at home in the palace. This notable museum contains wood and copper engravings by Dürer which the Wettins had started to collect as early as 1588. As the collection grew in size, Augustus the Strong had a special museum built to hold it. Today it contains 390,000 works, drawings and graphics dating back to 1400, together with historical portraits and views, photos, posters, and books.

The Art Library, also accommodated in the palace, contains around 130,000 volumes – with many recent works, but also several rare editions. With its countless decorations and early Renaissance elements, the Georgenbau already gives a foretaste of what the complex as a whole will look like when it is completed. The **"Beautiful Gate"** ("Schöne Tor") dating from 1555/56 has also been exquisitely renovated. Originally serving as the entrance to the Protestant Court Chapel, this portal has the appearance of a triumphal arch and is designed in a late Renaissance style. The Armoury has been rehoused within the palace's walls since 2013. It possesses a magnificent collection of ceremonial weapons that were used by Saxon princes at tournaments and hunts. Of particular note are the first electoral sword (1425), a decorative harness belonging to Elector Christian II and the coronation regalia of Augustus the Strong.

The stalls and Procession of Dukes (Fürstenzug) are described in greater detail later on.

"Delhi Court": Mir Miron's palanquin

Hofkirche ③

On the west side of the Schloss-platz is the Cathedral, the former Catholic Court Chapel (Hofkirche). Because of its oval form, the 83 metre bell tower changes in width, depending on the angle from which it is viewed, but it is always a dominant feature in the centre of the skyline, supported by the high roof of the nave and framed by no less

From the steps leading up to the Brühl Terrace, visitors have a fascinating view of the Catholic Hofkirche. To the left is the Hausmann Tower and the Georgenbau of the former Royal Palace.

than 78 statues of over 3 metres in height. The church was built in the mid-18th century by order of Augustus III under the direction of Italian architect Chiaveri who used his own countrymen exclusively for the building work. It is not oriented from West to East, as is normal with churches, but has its tower facing the bridge.

After his conversion to Catholicism – in order to become King of Poland – Augustus the Strong, who was little interested in religious matters, held Mass in the modest chapel in the Royal Palace until 1707, and then in the empty opera house within the palace. When the Protestant citizenry started building the Church of Our Lady (from 1726), the most important sacred Protestant building in Europe, Augustus realised the need to erect a Catholic equivalent. As there were evident difficulties, even for the king, in having a Catholic church built in a Protestant city, he had the plans and preparations for his Romanesque-Baroque structure made in secrecy. The religious compro-

Catholic Hofkirche: View of the famous organ, built by organ builder Gottfried Silbermann (1683–1753), through the three-storey high nave.

Interior of the Hofkirche: painting of the altar "The Ascension of Christ", on the right the pulpit by Permoser

mise which Augustus the Strong had accepted in 1697 also demanded that consideration be given to the Protestant inhabitants of the residential city who refused to recognise the church or allow its bells to ring. It was only in 1806 when Napoleon made Saxony into a kingdom that the bells pealed for the first time. The compromise is also evident inside the church which has a special aisle for processions. In Protestant Dresden a Catholic procession would have been inconceivable. The elaborate interior furnishings – a Silbermann organ, Rococo pulpit (Balthasar Permoser) and paintings by A.R. Mengs, who also worked in Madrid and Rome, provided a worthy setting for the new royal tombs. The Wettins from Henry the Pious onwards were buried in Freiberg cathedral which was out of bounds to the Catholic rulers. Augustus the Strong was laid to rest in the crypt of Krakow cathedral, but his heart was buried in the Dresden on completion of the Hofkirche. According to legend it is said to start beating even today every time a pretty woman passes by. It is kept in a plain copper vessel next to the more elaborate coffins of the Wettin princes.

After destruction in 1945 rebuilding of the church started in 1979 although it has still to be fully re-

Statue of St. Laurentius on the roof of the Court Chapel

stored. Of particular note is the faithful restoration of the organ, the largest and last work of the celebrated organ builder Gottfried Silbermann. A pieta made of Meissen porcelain (1975) in a side chapel is dedicated "to the victims of 13 February 1945 and all unjust violence". In 1980 a Papal decree designated the church as cathedral of the Bishopric of Dresden/Meissen.

Theaterplatz ④

Together with the palace the Hofkirche forms the east side of Theaterplatz, which is framed on all sides by sandstone buildings. On the Elbe side it is closed off by the low portals of the Italienisches Dörfchen restaurant, modestly bowing towards its grander neighbours. The name is derived from a collection of small buildings and rooms in which the Italian stonemasons were housed during the building of the Hofkirche. The present building was designed by Erlwein in 1912 in the New Baroque style typical of Dresden, while the statues were carved by G. Wrba.

Also in the square is the Old Town Watchtower (Altstädter Wache). Constructed by J. Thürmer (1830–32) from a design by K.F. Schinkel, it is notable for its very clean lines, with the gables being tastefully accented by the decorative sculptures. The centre of the square is dominated by a majestic equestrian statue erected in 1889 of the Saxon King John, who is also renowned for his translation of Dante's Divine Comedy.

Spring at Theaterplatz before the magnificent backdrop of the Hofkirche (left) and the former Royal Palace with the imposing Hausmann Tower

Semper Opera House ⑤

Dresden's fame as a music centre is due amongst other things to its theatres and opera houses, the most elegant and perfect of which dominates the Theaterplatz. An opera house already stood approximately on this site in 1678. It was one of the first permanent theatre buildings north of the Alps. It would be followed by eight additional opera houses. Famous conductors, composers, and singers worked in these opera houses: Heinrich Schütz, composer of the first German opera (Daphne), Johann Adolf Hasse, Carl Maria von Weber, and the Italian mezzo-soprano Bordoni. The new Royal Theatre was opened in 1841 and pushed its designer, Gottfried Semper, to the forefront of the European theatrical scene. The following year Richard Wagner came

The harmonious architecture of the Semper Opera House with its wide staircases at the side and the rhythm of its double columns and window arrangement, enhanced by the main portal in the form of a triumphal

to Dresden as conductor and conducted the first performances of his operas Rienzi, The Flying Dutchman, and Tannhäuser. Wagner and Semper became friends, fought together on the barricades for a democratic constitution, and had to flee Dresden following the failure of the revolution.

The magnificent building in the style of the early Italian Renaissance caught fire in 1869 and the opera moved to temporary premises, the Bretterbude, until 1878. Gottfried Semper was commissioned to design a new opera house. This busy architect had already designed the court theatre in Rio de Janeiro and the Festival Theatre in Munich (both of which, however, were never built) and was involved at the same time in planning the Kaiserforum and Burgtheater in Vienna. He nevertheless accepted this stimulating

arch with the crowning panther-drawn quadriga. The equestrian statue of King Johann of Saxony can be seen on the right.

Cross vault borne by the double columns and pilasters

The festive auditorium of Dresden Opera House

task and created the present edifice whose outer form, interior and functional design were to serve as a model for opera houses throughout the world. Famous conductors such as Karl Böhm have all worked here, and nine operas by Richard Strauss were performed for the first time in Dresden. The acoustics were even better than those in La Scala in Milan. During the air raids in February 1945 the opera house was reduced to rubble with the rest of the city centre and it took forty years before it was rebuilt with its largely original facade. The restoration of the interior has also been a great success. Visitors are again transported back to the heyday of opera, while the performers can make the most of modern technology. The site of the new Semper Opera house was set back a little, thus increasing the size of Theaterplatz and also enhancing the effect of the new structure. The front, with the door-like windows of the circular foyer, faces the centre of the square, the harmony of the whole being emphasised by the double columns in the upper storey. In the niches of the stairways at the sides are statues from the old Semper theatre, with Shakespeare and

Semper Opera House:
For guided tour enquiries, call
Tel. 0351 49110
www.semperoper.de

Sophocles on the left, and Molière and Euripides on the right. In the centre, the middle portal rises up like triumphal arch, crowned by a quadriga: Dionysus, Greek god of comedy and tragedy, steers his panther-drawn chariot with Ariadne at his side. Like the equestrian statue out front, this work comes from the studio of sculptor Johann Schilling. In the coloured niche underneath are the three Graces accompanied by Marsyas and Apollo. To the side of the main portal are the German poets Goethe and Schiller by Schilling's pupil Ernst Rietschel. The ornamentation on the recessed upper storeys is limited to plain windows and a few mythological figures on the antique gable of the fly tower, crowned by a symbolic lyre.

Inside the opera house is notable, despite the richly decorative and artistic ornaments, for its restrained elegance. The auditorium is in conventional form with stalls and boxes so that the audience is in perfect harmony with the surroundings and the works being performed. Equally impressive are the upper circular foyer and vestibule with their classical Renaissance festiveness.

The Theatre Square is dominated by the impressive façade of the Semper Opera House and evokes a feeling of romance in its bright evening glow.

Zwinger ⑥

The south side of Theaterplatz is formed by the neo-Renaissance facade of the Art Gallery. A memorial to the right commemorates the famous composer Carl Maria von Weber who was the director of the German opera in Dresden from 1817 to 1826. The middle passage leads through to the wide inner courtyard. With the exception of this Picture Gallery which was added later, the three-wing complex was built under Augustus the Strong from 1710 to 1732 in

View of the inner courtyard of the world-famous Zwinger with its

Baroque style. "Zwinger" derives its name from the site behind the town fortifications. Originally the King, who had been interested in his youth in architecture, designed the plan for the orangery himself. This temporary wooden structure was built in 1709. In 1710 Pöppel-mann was commissioned to design a permanent structure. He started the north-west section of the Zwinger with two double-storey corner pavilions and a single-storey arched gallery connecting the two buildings. The square became an open-air ballroom, an arena for parties

rampart pavilion, the artistically designed staircase

and receptions, unique of its kind in the world. The horizontal line is broken up by pavilions and gates with triumphal arches, emphasised by a succession of windows and arcades. Pöppelmann and his close collaborator, the sculptor Permoser, managed a perfect synthesis of architecture and sculptured ornamentation which made the Zwinger into a major attraction in a city which already had its fair share of notable buildings.

The main entrance and one of the landmarks of Dresden is the **Crown Gate** (Kronentor) whose gilded symbol of royal authority is borne by four Polish eagles. In the niches Permoser fitted statues representing the four seasons. The long gallery to the right leads to the **Salon of Mathematics and Physics** which

Zwinger: striking satyr's head

houses a zoological museum and a collection of scientific equipment, including fascinating old clocks. A harmoniously curved gallery con-

View of the courtyard of the Zwinger from the Langgalerie (Long Gallery)

The magnificent roof of the Crown Tower at the Zwinger

nects the building to the **Rampart Pavilion** (Wallpavillon) in which the symbiosis of architecture and sculpture is at its finest. The gatehouse serves exclusively as a wide staircase leading up to the arcades. The many statues are taken from the Greek myth of the Golden Apples of Hesperides. In order to obtain them Hercules had to carry the world on his shoulders, but employed a trick to relieve himself of the burden. The dome is crowned by a powerful male figure, "Hercules Saxonius" as Augustus the Strong liked to call it. To the right is the French Pavilion. In the build-ing to the left of the Crown Gate is the **porcelain collection** with valuable items from the Far East and from the Meissen factory, all in all one of the most extensive and impressive collections of its type in the world. Augustus the Strong paid the Prussian King Frederick William I for the famous Dragoon vases by giving him 600 of his dragoons. The exit on the city side leads to the **Carillon Pavilion** (Glockenspielpavillon) named after the carillon made of Meissen porcelain.

The side facing Theaterplatz remained open for more than 100 years after the death of Augustus,

Zwinger: the Salon of Mathematics and Physics houses a collection of scientific equipment

Porcelain Collection:
Salon of Mathematics and Physics:
Tue. – Sun. 10 am – 6 pm, Tel. 0351 49142000
www.skd.museum

Porcelain collection in the Zwinger: arched gallery with Chinese and Japanese porcelain

and the complex was also partially destroyed during the Seven Years' War. It was not until 1834 that Semper, then professor at the Art Academy, showed an interest again in the Zwinger. Originally he wanted to extend the building as far as the Elbe, incorporating his theatre, but the plan proved too expensive. In 1847 he began constructing what is today known as the Picture Gallery which closes off the courtyard and the complex without dominating Augustus's original buildings in any way. The western wing today houses the famous **Old Masters Gallery** (Gemäldegalerie

Carillon Pavilion

Alter Meister). This alone has attracted countless visitors to Dresden. How many galleries can boast such a large collection of top-class works by artists like Carregio, Titian (The Tribute Money), Gior-

The Bath of the Nymphs at the Zwinger is considered one of Permoser's most beautiful works of art.

Old Masters Gallery: the world-famous Sistine Madonna, a masterpiece by Italian artist Raphael (1483–1520)

gione (Sleeping Venus), Vermeer, Rembrandt, van Eyck, Lucas Cranach the Elder, and Albrecht Dürer, not to mention Raphael's world-famous Sistine Madonna which King Augustus III bought in 1754 for the enormous sum of 20,000 ducats. Climbing from the Rampart Pavilion the visitor reaches an arcade which offers a magnificent view of

Art Gallery "Old Masters":
Tue. – Sun. 10 am – 6 pm, Tel. 0351 49142000
www.skd.museum

For his mistress, Countess Cosel, August the Strong had Taschenberg Palace built adjacent to the Palace.

the entire Zwinger complex. The missing statues and decorative elements show how much restoration work still needs to be done. Behind the French Pavilion to the right of the staircase can be seen a collection of sculptures which go to make up one of Permoser's major works, the **Bath of the Nymphs** (Nymphenbad). In each of the niches eight delightful nymphs regard the artistic fountains, themselves secretly observed by satyrs, demons and fish-like monsters. The lively scene around the waterfall symbolises the sensuality of the Baroque era which Augustus's sculptor Permoser has so masterfully immortalised.

Taschenberg Palace ⑦ and Cholera Fountain

Passing through the Carillon Pavilion, opposite the staircase tower of the Rampart Pavilion, we leave the Zwinger. On the other side of the road is the Taschenberg Palace, which Augustus the Strong had built in 1706 for his most famous mistress, Countess Cosel. Today it is an exclusive hotel with a vaulted cellar that has been turned into a magnificent medieval restaurant. Augustus's weakness for the fairer sex was well known – he even had an underground passage built that connected the building directly with the Royal Palace. The ambitious countess managed to wring a promise of marriage from the king and enjoyed a certain amount of political influence in the court, which naturally created enemies for her. In 1716 she fell from grace and was able to escape, only to be captured and exchanged for Prussian deserters. She spent the remaining 49 years of her life imprisoned in a tower at Stolpen Castle. The palace later became the residence of the elector's family and was modified and extended several times. After 1945 it was used mainly as an office building. The ruin has been restored as befits its historical tradition and was re-opened as a hotel in 1994. Apart from the facade with its decorative relief in the entrance area, the staircase and some rooms have been reconstructed in their original form.

After the Opera and Zwinger gallery, Semper gave Dresden a further monument, the Cholera Fountain in front of the Taschenberg Palace. Unlike his more famous Renaissance-style buildings, he designed this monument, most effectively, in Gothic style. The 18 metre structure resembles a church spire. It commemorates the cholera epidemic of 1840/41 whose ravages thankfully left Dresden unscathed.

Old Marketplace ⑧ (Altmarkt)

Turning from Taschenberg Palace into Kleine Brüdergasse and from there into Schlossstrasse in the direction of the Old Marketplace, we can see on the left, in Wilsdruffer Strasse, the Cultural Palace with its copper roof, built in 1966–69. With a ground plan of 102 by 70 metres, it offers plenty of room for events of all kinds. The Festsaal, where the Dresden Philharmonic often performs, can seat 2,400 visitors.

Detail of the Cholera Fountain, built from a design by Semper dated 1843

In front of the **Cultural Palace** is the vast expanse of Old Marketplace, a smaller version of which already existed more than five hundred years ago. Only the Holy Cross Church remained of the buildings erected before 1945, however. In the 1950s work started on reconstructing the east and west sides of the historical square. The houses were designed in the traditional Baroque style of Dresden. From 1741 to 1945 the Old Town Hall stood on the west side of the square. Prior to 1741 there had been a town hall opposite the site of the Cultural Palace, before August the Strong had it demolished in 1707 to make space for a parade ground.

In a building on the west side is the well-known Café Prag, while the east side faces the **Holy Cross Church** which until 1945 was outside square, in those days much smaller than now. Even before the town was chartered a place of worship, St Nicholas Church, was to be found here. It changed its name after the marriage of Henry the Illustrious (13th century) whose wife brought a relic from the Cross with her. After 1400 it was rebuilt in Gothic style, only to be destroyed again in the fire of 1491. Its successors in later centuries suffered

Until 1878 the Holy Cross Church on the Old Marketplace was the mother church of the world-famous Church of Our Lady.

New Town Hall: the 98 m high tower with its "Golden Man" dominates this compact, functional building. In the background, the top of the Holy Cross Church

similar fates through fire and warfare. The present church was built around 1900 and restored after 1945 to give the famous choir – Kreuzchor a suitable and worthy setting in which to perform.

To the north of the church is Kreuzstrasse in the shadow of the massive, slightly disorganised **New Town Hall** ⑨, originally built between 1905 and 1910. The south wing and Festsaal wing in the east were rebuilt in simplified form in 1948–52 and 1962–65 respectively. The "Golden Man" is visible far and wide at the top of the 100 metre tower with its tapering two-section copper dome. On the viewing tower are works of renowned sculptors such as Peter Pöppelmann, Fischer, Selbmann and Steinmüller. Georg Wrba's bronze casting "Bacchus on a Donkey" at the entrance to the Ratskeller is also much admired. One of the wine god's toes remains permanently polished as passing visitors touch it for luck.

Continuing along Rathausplatz past the Trümmerfrau we come to the Gewandhaus, erected in 1768–70 from designs by J.G. Schmidt and F. Knöbel. This Baroque building was also destroyed during the war and rebuilt as a hotel in 1965–67.

Of particular interest is the Dinglinger Fountain at the rear of the building, where it was moved in 1966 from the ruins of Dinglinger's house. Close by, in Weisse Gasse, is another fountain, the Goose Thief from a design by F.A. Krubsacius. The Classicist facade was the first of its type in Dresden. The impressive double-flight staircase and magnificent wrought iron banisters are well worth looking at. The

The Landhaus, today the Historical Museum of the City of Dresden

Fountain (Gänsediebbrunnen), built in 1876–80 by Robert Diez, which was also moved here from its original location.

Landhaus ⑩

Walking back to the Dinglinger Fountain and along Gewandhausstrasse we can see on the other side of the wide Wilsdruffer Strasse the Landhaus, built in 1770 – 76 Landhaus was completely restored in 1963–65 and listed as a historic monument. Today it houses the Museum of the City of Dresden whose four storeys contain many exhibits relating to the history of the city and state, providing an insight into the evolution of the city from its founding to the present day. Opposite the north facade of the Landhaus is the police presidium in Schiessgasse, built in 1895– 1900 by architect J. Temper in the

City Gallery/City Museum at the Manor House:
Sat. – Tue. 10 am – 6 pm, Fri. 10 am – 7 pm
Monday closed, Tel. 0351 4887360
www.museen-dresden.de

style of a Renaissance palace with Baroque flourishes. Facing it is the Kurländer Palace, built in 1729 by J.Ch. Knöffel for Minister Wackerbarth. The palace is named after a later owner, the Duke of Kurland.

a magnificent four-winged Neo-Renaissance structure was erected. For art lovers the building is one of the most important in Dresden as it houses museums of considerable significance, such as the Gallery of

Staircase in the Old Landhaus

Albertinum ⑪

Tzschirnerplatz separates the colossal police presidium from the equally massive and recently restored sandstone Albertinum. It was built on order of King Albert in 1884 upon the foundations of the former arsenal (16th century). Of this building the two-aisled columned hall in the ground floor remains, over which

19th and 20th Century Painters (Galerie "Neue Meister") and the extensive collection of sculptures.

The Gallery of 19th and 20th Century Painters was separated in 1931 from the Picture Gallery which had become unmanageably large. It shows works of all styles from Classicist and Impressionist to Socialist art from the 19th and 20th centuries. Paintings by Romantics such as C.D. Friedrichs and Ludwig Richter are particularly popular, but works by Manet, Monet, Degas, Gauguin, Van Gogh, Max Liebermann and Otto Dix also have their place here.

The entrance to these collections is located at Georg-Treu-Platz. From here it is also possible to reach the second museum in the Albertinum, the **sculpture collection.** Through the purchase of antique marble sculptures Augustus the Strong laid the foundations for the present

Albertinium: facade of the museum building (from 1884) in front of Brühl Garden. It houses two museums.

Art Gallery,
Collection of sculptures:
Tue. – Sun. 10 am – 6 pm, Tel. 0351 49142000
www.skd.museum

museum which contains around 500 sculptures, mostly Roman copies of Greek originals. There are also sculptures, vases and objets d'art from ancient Egypt, the Near East, Greece, Etruria, and a collection of European sculptures from the early Middle Ages to modern times.

Georg-Treu-Platz is the starting point for guided visits for the **casemates** under the former remparts, which was part of the defense system of the town against attacks from the Elbe.

New Marketplace ⑫ (Neumarkt)

The northern boundary of the reconstructed Church of Our Lady (Frauenkirche) is marked by the **Royal Art Academy** (Kunstakademie, 1891). This building complex is overlooked by a glass dome, crowned with a gold-plated allegory of Fama (Pheme). The roof which is part of Dresden's skyline along the River Elbe is jokingly referred to by the locals as the "lemon press".

Opposite, the **"Cosel Palace"** ⑬ in Baroque yellow catches the eye with its two-storey wings.

Count Cosel, son of Augustus the Strong, and his famous mistress, erected the five-storey edifice with the rounded grille and the lively putti groups in 1762.

Until 1945 the Church of Our Lady was surrounded by a very harmonious quarter which formed a striking contrast to the buildings of the Saxon Court. These houses are currently been restored following original plans.

Pompous Palace of Countess Cosel at the New Marketplace

The Church of Our Lady (Frauenkirche) ⑭

Already at the beginning of the 18th century there was here a "Church of Our Lady", which in the course of the years had been more and more in danger of falling and also become too small for the increased number of protestant inhabitants. Therefore, in 1726 the city of Dresden decided to rebuild the imposing church as a symbol of their protestant convictions and as a display of protest against the absolutism of the prince elector Augustus the Strong and his con-

The rebuilt church of Our Lady is a unique example of baroque Saxon architecture.

The bells of the Church of Our Lady before being fitted

The 4.70 m high tower cross crowning the Church of Our Lady is a donation of the British association "Dresden Trust".

The ruin of the famous Church of Our Lady as it looked before reconstruction started in 1993.

Panoramic view of the interior of the church with the altar and the new organ

version to catholicism. Town master carpenter, George Bähr, was commissioned to superintend one of the most important masterpieces of architecture in Europe. This huge strong-man act, which required almost 30000 thalers, was financed using the town treasury and thanks to donations of Dresden inhabitants. In order to reduce the costs, Bähr utilized the sandstone of the previous construction and planned a wood dome. Only thanks to a considerable donation of prince elector Augustus III, son and successor of Augustus the Strong, it was possible to build the imposing "stone bell" using sandstone. With an external diameter of 26 metres it is the biggest stone dome north of the Alps. The external "shell" is up to 1,75 m thick,

The Church of our Lady:
Opening hours s. notice, climbing of the tower: Mar. – Oct. Mon. – Sat. 10 am – 6 pm, Sun. 12:30 pm – 6 pm, Nov. – Feb. Mon. – Sat. 10 am – 4 pm, Sun. 12:30 pm – 4 pm, www.frauenkirche-dresden.de

whereas the internal one is 25 cm thick. Between the two coatings there is a spiral ambulatory which leads to the 68 metres high panoramic platform. The dome, included the "lantern", weighs 13000 tons, whereas the cross is more than 91 metres high.

Two days after the terrible air-raid in February 1945 the Church of Our Lady collapsed completely. The burning houses had produced a huge heat of more than 1000° C, which had set on fire the pews inside the church and caused the sandstone to crumble.

Even if soon after 1945 the reconstruction of the church had been already planned, it was necessary to renounce to it due to lack of money. Therefore, the remains, a heap of ruins with two bigger wall parts, stayed unchanged till 1993, as a memorial against the foolishness of war and of absurd destruction. Also after the reconstruction of the church a large number of Dresden inhabitants remember the victims of war every year on 13th February placing burning candles and praying. During the last months before the fall of Berlin wall the square was the place of speechless understanding and of the rising protest against the unpopular regime.

View of the interior with the galleries and the altar

After the reunification a group of 14 persons, under the direction of the musician Ludwig Güttler, founded "Dresden's Cry", which was looking for funds for the reconstruction of the Church of Our Lady all around the world. From this group Germany's biggest action of monuments protection and of citizens' initiative was born, also supported by four associations in Great Britain, United States, France and Switzerland. Initiatives such as "adoptions of stones", sale of watches and souvenirs with fragments of the ruins, commemorative coins and donators' letters increased the amount of the donations, so that in 1993 it was possible to begin removing the rubble. More than 7000 pieces were found, among which a 95 tons heavy copper plate belonging to the tower façade and important rests of the high altar. All these pieces were registered in computer, numbered and stored on big shelves in order to reuse them later on. Only for the façade it was thus possible to reutilize 3539 pieces, which today can be easily recognized thanks to their dark patina. In fact, today the church is made for 45% of original pieces.

Detail of the altar – the praying Christ in front of Jerusalem outline

View of the Art Academy and of the Church of Our Lady

The façade was completed in 2004 with the lantern, crowned by a 6 metres high gilded cross set on the symbol of the terrestrial globe. It is the donation of the British association "Dresden Trust", among whose members there are important personalities such as the duke of Kent and the bishop of Coventry. The cross was sent to Dresden by the queen herself in an official ceremony and handed over by the duke of Kent. Also the son of a British bomber pilot taking part in Dresden air-raid contributed to the preparations. Important donators can also be found in the successful American association "Friends of Dresden": the former Foreign Minister Henry A. Kissinger and David Rockefeller as patrons and the Nobel prize, professor Günter Blobel as president, who allocated a big part of his prize to the reconstruction of the Church of Our Lady. These are promising signs of reconciliation among former war enemies.

A big piece of ruins was placed on the north side of the church, near the main entrance. It is part of the external "shell" of the dome of the collapsed church. Its original position is explained in the inscription and in a church view.

The interior impresses at first because of its gigantic dimensions: the pillars are 18 metres high, the internal dome is almost 40 m high in its highest point, 1835 persons can seat on the church pews. The balustrades of the sweeping galleries as well as the pillars have returned to their brilliant rosé, blue, green and yellow tones like in 1743, during the baroque age. Especially here it becomes clear why only the construction costs of this successful restoration amount to the considerable sum of 132 million Euro.

For Dresden tourists the symbolic church of Our Lady should be first of all a place of meditation in the middle of the uproar of the lively and crowded old town. At the same time it is an ecumenical meeting place, where religious services and prayers are celebrated. Moreover, it offers an overwhelming background to cultural events and concerts of sacred music.

If it is nice, it is worth climbing up to the 68 m high panoramic platform on the church dome. The first half is not strenuous because it is possible to take the lift. Some steps follow as well as the 160 metres long ambulatory between the external and the internal coatings of the dome, before getting to the last steps and to the platform with balustrade. All these efforts are rewarded by a wonderful view of Dresden old town as well as of the suburbs on this side and on the other side of the Elbe.

View of the Church of Our Lady from Brühl Terrace.
On the right the dome of the Art Academy

The Church of Our Lady at the New Marketplace,

(painting by Bernardo Belotto entitled "Canaletto", dating from 1749)

The former Royal Stables, the "Johanneum", with its imposing steps, is used today as a transport museum.

Procession of Dukes ⑮ in the Stable Courtyard

The west side of the New Marketplace is formed by the main building of the former royal stables, the **Johanneum**. The front faces the Jüdenhof. The double-flight staircase, known as the English Staircase, was built in Baroque style in the reign of Augustus the Strong, while the side round-arched portals date from the 16th century. The upper storey with its high round-arched windows was designed by Knöffel in 1875. The nearby Turkish Fountain (Türkenbrunnen) was built in 1648 to mark the end of the Thirty Years' War but was renamed in 1683 and topped by a statue of Viktoria to commemorate the services of Elector John George III in relieving Vienna from siege by the Turks.

Transport Museum:
Tue. – Sun. 10 am – 6 pm, Tel. 0351 86440
www.verkehrsmuseum-dresden.de

The main building was originally used as a stable. It was converted in 1856 to a picture gallery until the gallery in the Zwinger was completed. The name Johanneum dates from this time when King John

Picturesque entrance ▶ to the Stable Courtyard

▼ *Langer Gang (1586–91) and Johanneum, former royal stables*

commissioned it as a historical museum and armoury. Since its reconstruction in 1958 it has housed the Transport Museum which documents the history of transportation on land, sea and air. Apart from an extensive collection of bicycles, the Muldenthal steam engine (1861), the oldest existing tram in Germany, and the first successful motorised aeroplane in the world (1909) have real scarcity value for old-timer fans. The round-arched arcades of the **Langer Gang** (long passage) are

Procession of Princes: a monumental mosaic made of Meissen porcelain tiles showing the rulers of the house of Wettin.

amongst the only part of the former royal palace which were restored before reunification. They connect the Johanneum with the Georgenbau, the centre of the palace complex. The Stable Courtyard was erected at the end of the 16th century and was used, as its name suggests, for housing the horses. The arches above the Tuscan arcades are decorated by hunting trophies and three-dimensional coats-of-arms of the Saxon estates. Scraped stucco ornaments adorn the walls

At the end, the tower of the George Gate and the Hofkirche.

above and below the rhythmically arranged windows of the upper storey. The 100 m yard is the oldest jousting arena in Europe. The four bronze columns, for example, are part of a ring-tilting course used in tournaments. From the courtyard a ramp used to lead to the upper storey of the stables which could thus be reached on horseback. During the yuletide "Striezelmarkt", a medieval spectacle attracts thousands of visitors here.

The sides of the Langer Gang are also interesting. Together with the Ständehaus they form a shaded passageway through the narrow Augustusstrasse, ending with the high facade of the Hofkirche. In 1870–76 the artist Wilhelm Walter painted the 102-metre **Procession of Dukes**, a parade of rulers of the house of Saxe-Wettin. The original work was in scratched stucco but after damage quickly became visible the monumental painting was covered in 1906 with 25,000 Meissen porcelain tiles. It survived the air raids of 1945 and documents the thousand year history of the house of Wettin, together with the clothing and weapons of the different epochs. A total of 35 margraves, electors and kings – on horseback – are portrayed, in most cases with the dates of their reigns and their nicknames. There was "the Strong", "the Rich", "the Warlike" and "the Gentle", "the Kind", "the Proud", "the Illustrious", and even "the Stubborn". Between and behind them are the rank and file: heralds, guards and standard bearers, servants,

moors, children scattering flowers, and representatives of science and the arts. The "only" persons missing are the female members of the family, who were ignored not only in the painting but also in the royal line of succession.

Brühl Terrace ⑯

At the end of Augustusstrasse we arrive back at the start of our tour, namely the southern end of Augustus Bridge. Here a monumental staircase (1814) leads up to Brühl Terrace, flanked by four bronze groups symbolising the times of the day, from the studio of Schilling. Morning, top left, is recognisable by the morning star on the forehead of the female figure and the welcoming gesture. Midday is represented by a corona, Evening shows a family singing and making music together, while Night is a mother with a robe to protect her child and an angel whispering dreams in its ear.

The end of the staircase is at the height of the former ramparts facing the Elbe which were erected to protect the city. These ramparts were gradually acquired by Count Henry von Brühl, prime minister under Augustus the Strong, who had the terrace laid out in accordance with plans of the renowned Baroque architect J. Chr. Knöffel to form what Goethe called "the balcony of Europe". At the time, however, the magnificent residence of the duke, demolished and replaced at the end of the 19th century, was still standing. The former Brühl Palace was also affected, and had to make way for the construction of new state parliament house, since the old state parliament house was no longer big enough. Paul Wallot

by Johannes Schilling.

The former state parliament was gutted by fire in 1945 and now, after partial restoration, houses the Museum for Mineralogy and Geology and the German Photothek. It

A stroll along the famous Brühl Terrace is a must for every visitor to Dresden. On the left is the tower of the former state parliament building, today the Superior State Court, and behind it the Hofkirche. On the right is the Rietschel Memorial.

was commissioned with this project. His initial plan to preserve Brühl Palace and include it in the new building could not be realised for a number of reasons. The new four-winged state parliament building or Ständehaus was built 1900–1907. The small tower figure, "Saxonia" is

is also home to the Superior State Court of the Free State of Saxony. The building itself, with its high roof spire, set back in the direction of the bridge, fits in well with the Dresden skyline and the architecture of the Royal Palace and Hofkirche.

The beige plaster of the **Sekundo-genitur**, palace for the second-born son of the ruling couple, makes a bright and friendly impression. The Brühl library, which once contained more than 60,000 volumes, had to give way in 1897 to this Neo-Baroque building. After the end of the monarchy it served as a gallery, and since its reconstruction in 1964 it has been used as a restaurant.

In front of the facade J. Schilling eternalised his master, Ernst Rietschel, in a memorial erected in 1875 on the site of the former Brühl garden pavilion which Rietschel had used as a studio. Next to it is a modern bronze casting symbolising the globe. The inscription on the terrace floor refers to a decree by Augustus the Strong of 1721 that the seven bastions of the royal and electoral residential city should be named after the planets (in those days including Sol – the sun – and Luna – the moon). The Münzgasse below the terrace is a busy place already afternoons, for it is home to the old city bar district. On the terrace, however, is the royal Art Academy with its exhibition room rich in ornamental sculptures and with a mighty portal whose gable relief was sculpted by J. Schilling. A multi-storey masonry shaft on the side of the terrace that faces the Elbe affords a glimpse of one of the mightiest casements in the city. At this place, a "mouth hole" permitted barges to travel between the stream that at that time flowed around the outer wall of the fortifications and the fortification system (1545 – 53). Four cannons and additional heavy weapons were deployed to defend the "mouth hole". Where the double-flight staircase opens onto Georg-Treu-Platz we find the Semper memorial, another work by Schilling. It shows the architect with a building plan of his first theatre in Dresden. This brings us back to the Albertinum with its

Façade of the Art Academy opposite the Brühl Terrace

Evening atmosphere at Brühl Terrace. In the foreground is the lovely façade of the Sekundogenitur; behind it is the Art Academy with its distinctive cupola.

slanting front which, together with the narrow terrace, forms the triangular Brühl Garden, under which the **Virgin Bastion** (Jungferbastei) of the medieval fortifications was hidden. On this site until 1747 stood the famous summerhouse in the cellar of which the alchemist Böttger ran a laboratory together with von Tschirnhaus and in which he made his sensational discovery of European porcelain. Only the Dolphin Fountain (1748) and the two sphinx groups on high pedestals remain of the Baroque buildings. On the spur of the garden facing the city a light, bourgeois Baroque plaster structure, the former court nursery (1752), fits neatly into the complex. Under the red roof with its eyebrows, the Reform Community of Dresden holds its services today, while another part of the building serves as an old people's home. At the back of the building is a column commemorating the victims of Fascism in the Third Reich and marking the site of the synagogue of 1838, wantonly destroyed 100 years later. In the meantime, the Jewish community has built a new **synagogue** ⑰ opposite, where the Semper Synagogue once stood. The new synagogue, constructed on the model of the first Israelite temple, takes the form of a windowless cube with a prayer room that faces east, which is emphasised in the way that the layers of stones are oriented. Tons of glass shards and concrete blocks are a symbolic reminder of what was hopefully the last period of suffering ever for Jews in Germany.

If we walk along the wall to the bastion spur facing the Elbe we discover the epitaph-like **Maurice Monument** ⑱ (Moritzmonument), the oldest monument in Dresden. In 1547 Duke Maurice became elector of his Protestant state. The 32-year-old Elector was fatally wounded during the battle of Sievershausen on 9 July 1553 in which he defeated Margrave Albert Alcibiades of Brandenburg. The memorial shows the dying man handing the electoral sword to his brother Augustus, the two wives at his side. The scene surrounded by columns was created by the famous Renaissance sculptor H. Walther II.

As we return to Schlossplatz – at the foot of the terrace or, even better, on it – we can cast a glance at the north bank of the Elbe with the massive buildings of the former Saxon general ministries, right, and the finance ministry. Both were built around 1900 as four-wing Neo-Baroque structures. On the banks of Altstadt are berthed the ships of the Weisse Flotte, half of which are still steam-driven. The oldest steamer, a paddle steamer and the most popular amongst the people of Dresden, is the Diesbar. It was built in England in 1883. Its paddle wheels are driven by a steam engine built in 1857, the oldest working engine still in service in the world. Since 1980 it has been listed as a technical monument. The larger of the moored ships are used as floating hotels and help to alleviate the current shortage of accommodation in Dresden.

Monument to Duke Maurice who obtained the status of Electorate for Saxony in 1547

Morning sun on the Elbe; view of the ministerial buildings from the steps of Brühl Terrace.

Tour of Neustadt

The central Augustus Bridge leads to the former "Altendresden" which burnt down completely in 1685 and has been known since its reconstruction as Neustadt (new town). At the time von Klengel was the royal architect in the service of the Saxon electors. He had been summoned to the court in 1656 by Elector John George II, grandfather of Augustus the Strong, to direct the building work on the Royal Palace and also to train future architects and the young princes. Matthäus Pöppelmann, subsequently to become famous in his own right, and the young Augustus, later to be known as "the Strong", received basic instruction in architecture from him. This training is seen by experts as the clue to the high quality of Dresden's Baroque architecture. The various building decrees issued by von Klengel and Pöppelmann concerning the form and height of buildings go a long way to explaining the much admired harmony of the urban architecture, particularly in Neustadt. After becoming King of Poland in 1696, Augustus the Strong commissioned Pöppelmann to make Dresden into a city of international rank, a "Venice on the Elbe". He also contributed several ideas of his own, although not all of them could be implemented, due to financial constraints.

At the north end of the bridge Augustus had a massive building (Blockhaus) constructed to replace the old arsenal. It was to be crowned by a **gilded equestrian statue (Goldener Reiter)** ⑲ showing the ruler in Roman armour. This landmark of the city now stands on its high pedestal on the Neustadter marketplace. This is where the Dresden's main street (Hauptstrasse) starts. Although little is left of the original Baroque buildings that used to line it, the tree-bordered avenue, with its Baroque statues, is still one of the most elegant streets in the city. Fortunately, some of the Baroque buildings at the far end of the street were spared during the bombing – such as no. 13, the **Kügelgen House**, which derives its name from the painter Gerhard von Kügelgen who lived here from 1808 onwards. Prominent visitors of the time included Caspar David Friedrich, Carus, Goethe, Körner and Kleist. The building now houses the Dresden Museum of Early Romanticism with furniture and mementoes of the period.

Not far from the Kügelgen House is the **Church of the Epiphany** ⑳, which, on the instructions of Augustus the Strong, was to be assim-

The gilded equestrian statue (1736) of Augustus the Strong, Elector of Saxony and King of Poland

Dresden Museum of Early Romanticism:
Kügelgen House, Wed. – Sun. 10 am – 6 pm, Tel. 0351 8044760
www.museen-dresden.de

The delightful Baroque facades in Neustadt main street remained unscathed by the air raids of the Second World War.

ilated into the overall urban landscape. Its predecessor, which had only be erected in 1685 following the fire, was demolished in 1732 to make way for the new rectangular church. Of particular note are the 7 m sandstone altar and 12 m long sandstone frieze, the Dresden Dance of Death. This impressive work was created in 1535 by local Renaissance sculptor Christroph Walther I and was originally located in the Georgenbau of the Royal Palace.

The Three Magi Church – Baroque church between Hauptstraße and Königstraße

Fountain "Troubled Waters" at Albertplatz

Hauptstrasse ends at **Albertplatz** ㉑. Here, in the centre of Neustadt, there are two eye-catching monumental fountains, called "Still Waters" and "Troubled Waters" respectively. They are from the studio of Robert Diez and began sharing this site again in 1994. There is another interesting fountain nearby, an artesian well, the pavilion-type housing of which was designed by Municipal Building Inspector Hans Erlwein in 1911. Many Dresden residents come here to take the healthful spring water.

The ancient-style pavilion fountain at Albertplatz (Albert Square) belongs to the artesian well, which still flows today.

In the extension of the Hauptstrasse on the other side of Albert Square, we turn into Alaunstrasse, which leads us to the outer part of Neustadt. This is the largest preserved Victorian-era neighbourhood in Europe, with richly varied facades, little galleries, theatres, and shops. Eccentric cafes and hundreds of trendy bars, often with earthy backyards and outside seating, draw scores of young and young-minded people to this neighbourhood night after night. A special magnet for visitors is the **"Art Passage"** ㉒ , which starts at Alaunstrasse 70 and leads to Gör-litzer Strasse (Nos. 21–25). It starts with the "Courtyard of the Fantastic Creatures", fashioned of tile shards, leads on through the "Courtyard of Light" (outsized mirrors) to the "Courtyard of the Elements" (dynamic sheets on a façade the colour of the golden sun, with elaborately installed gutters on a water-blue façade opposite), the puzzling "Courtyard of the Metamorphoses", and, finally, the "Courtyard of the Animals", representations of which reel between treehouse-like balconies.

Here we leave the art passage for Görlitzer Strasse, which we follow

Many of the numerous "in"-bars in the Victorian era neighbourhood in the outer part of Neustadt offer their patrons atmospheric outdoor seating in summer.

*A fascinating composition with rain gutters on one of the façades
in the Art Passage*

Pfund's dairy: the most beautiful dairy in the world, in Bautzner Straße, not far from Albertplatz (Albert Square). Extraordinary representation of

the history of milk production depicted in the coloured tiles.

to the right until we turn left on Louisenstrasse and later right onto Martin-Luther-Strasse. This route leads us to the similarly named square and church. At the back, slightly off to the left, is the atmospheric Old Jewish Cemetery, in which more than a thousand members of the Jewish community were laid to rest between 1751 and 1869. Walking past the East side of the church again, we come to a broad street called Bautzner Strasse, onto which we turn left. House No. 79 is a special jewel amongst Dresden's many attractions: **Pfund's Dairy** ㉓, established in 1891. Since 1997 – according to the Guinness Book of World Records, it is entitled to call itself the "prettiest dairy in the world", decorated with nearly 250 square metres of hand painted tiles.

Hand-painted tiles

The famous Pfund's Angel

Königstraße – the most prestigious street in Dresden

Augustus the Strong intended the Japanese Palace to hold his collection of Oriental and Meissen porcelain.

Bautzener Strasse leads us – westward – straight back to Albert Square in the centre of Neustadt. On the west side of the square, at Antonstr. 1, an association of backers has set up a museum dedicated to Dresden author Erich Kästner (1899–1974), author of famous books for young people such as "Lisa and Lottie" and "Emil and the Detectives". The latest media technology is put to impressive use, enabling visitors of all ages to playfully discover the author's world for themselves.

On the way back to the Elbe, the Schiller monument marks the entrance to Königstrasse. The decoratively renovated town houses invite one to window shop and visit one of the many pubs. The numerous atmospheric backyards, in particular, are a continual attraction for visitors who prefer a special flair. Even during the cooler part of the year, it is well worth venturing a glance behind the facades of the street front. At the end of Königsstrasse we find Palaisplatz and, off to the right, we can see the Classicist columned **Akzisehaus**. It is one of two identical buildings erected by Thormeyer in the square from 1827 to 1829. The name points to the former tollhouse that stood here.

State Museum of Ethnology: *Tue.–Sun. 10 am–6 pm, Tel. 0351 8144860*
Senckenberg Natural History Collection Dresden: *Tue.–Sun. 10 am–6 pm, Tel. 0351 7958414326, www.senckenberg.de*
Museum of Prehistory: *Tue.–Sun. 10 am–6 pm, Tel. 0351 8926603*

Diagonally opposite is the **Japanese Palace** ㉔ built between 1715 and 1717 in quasi-Asian style with characteristic roofs on the corner pavilions. The reference to Oriental architecture is even more apparent in the gable relief in which Chinese and Saxon figures hand porcelain vessels to Saxonia sitting on her throne, or in the herms in the inner courtyard which have evident Chinese features. The building was acquired by Augustus the Strong in 1717 and was used by him to display his porcelain collection. The interiors, including the ceilings, were to be furnished exclusively in Chinese and Meissen porcelain. This plan was forgotten following the death of Augustus. The edifice, which is still in need of repair, serves as a venue for temporary exhibitions on various themes organised by the museums of ethnology (Museum für Völkerkunde), zoology and pre- and early history.

Sprawling behind the monument is a well manicured park with old trees and a vantage point looking down onto the Elbe promenade. The mound offers a delightful view of the banks of Altstadt with the Mosque-like former cigarette factory. We return to Augustus Bridge either along the Elbe promenade or by way of Grosse Meissner Strasse. On the way we pass the modern facade of a luxury hotel with an elegant Baroque building, the **Old Chancellery** (Alte Kanzlei) built ca. 1700, at its centre. In the 18th century this building used to house government departments and was later used as offices. It was the only one of many Baroque buildings in this street to survive the bombing of 1945. From the Elbe side of the Old Chancellery Canaletto painted the silhouette of the city in the mid-18th century, today famous throughout the world as a delightful representation of this "Florence on the Elbe".

Beyond the Neustadter marketplace, with its gilded equestrian statue, is a further interesting building, the **Jägerhof** ㉕ , on the north side of

Old Chancellery made famous by the Italian artist Canaletto who painted a silhouette of Dresden from here in the 18th century.

Köpckestrasse, opposite the Ministry of Finance. With its original Renaissance gable and three staircase towers it is the oldest surviving building in Neustadt. After serving as a menagerie for exotic animals under Augustus the Strong and a cavalry barracks in the 19th

Christmas lanterns and angels, pyramids and cribs originating in the Erzgebirge.

Around 3 km to the north of Augustus Bridge is Dr.-Kurt-Fischer-Platz with its **Military History Museum** (Militärhistorisches Museum) in the former arsenal where

Jägerhof, the oldest building in Neustadt, served as a menagerie for exotic animals under Augustus the Strong.

century, and after having been partially demolished, it housed the **Museum for Arts and Crafts** (Museum für Volkskunst), the first of its kind in Germany, from 1913 onwards. A total of 27,000 exhibits show the culture of peasants, craftsmen and miners: traditional costumes, painted furniture, stoneware, ribbon weaving, toys and much more. Of particular interest are the

weapons and armour of the Saxon rulers were kept until the outbreak of the First World War. Today more than 6,000 exhibits, from a Renaissance field harnesses to a modern tank, can be examined at leisure in the indoor exhibition rooms and outside.

About 5km further north, on the edge of Dresden Heath, the suburb of **Hellerau** sprung up in 1906 as

Museum of Saxon Folk Art with Puppet Theatre Collection:
Jägerhof, Tue. – Sun. 10 am – 6 pm, Tel. 0351 49144502
www.skd.museum
Museum of Military History: *Thu. – Tue. 10 am – 6 pm,*
Mon. 10 am – 9 pm, Tel. 0351 8232803, www.mhmbw.de

Museum of Military History with the Libeskind Wedge

Germany's first garden city. The German workshops created here have since been refurbished and extended. The theatre created by an architect by the name of Tessenow has once again become an attraction for avant-garde artists from all over the world.

Hellerau: Am Grünen Zipfel

Hellerau Festival Hall (Festspielhaus)

The Yenidze ㉖ ,
*a former tobacco
factory in the form
of a mosque with a
stained glass dome*

Dresden outside Altstadt

The Tobacco Mosque marks the boundary of Altstadt and Friedrichstadt. In the crypt of St Michael's Church is the tomb of Zwinger architect Pöppelmann. Not far away on the same side of the street is **Brühl Palace**, also known as **Marcolini Palace**. The oldest building in this complex was constructed in 1728 by Augustus the Strong for his mistress Princess von Teschen. In 1736 it was acquired as a country seat and considerably enlarged by Count Henry von Brühl, after whom Brühl Terrace is named. Behind the palace a large French-style garden was laid out with the imposing Neptune Fountain which remains the most impressive Baroque fountain in Dresden today. In the centre of the 40 m wide fountain are colossal stone statues of Poseidon and his wife Amphitrite. The complex was enlarged even further by Count C. Marcolini, director of the Meissen Porcelain Factory from 1774 onwards and later also Director General of the Art Academy. While he was still alive Napoleon met here with Austria's foreign minister Count Metternich in 1813. Richard Wagner occupied part of the palace between 1847 and 1849 and wrote Lohengrin. Other famous personalities are buried in the **Inner Catholic Cemetery** ㉗ : the opera composer Carl Maria von Weber, the sculptor B. Permoser, the painter von Kügelgen, the poet von Schlegel, and the Chevalier de Saxe, son of Augustus the Strong and Princess von Teschen.

The next Elbe bridge west of Friedrichstadt leads us to Übigau which contains **Übigau Palace**, one of Augustus the Strong's riverside residences. The wide stairway of this Baroque structure leads down to the river, enabling the ruler to reach the palace by gondola. Built around 1725, it was frequently the venue of court festivities and fireworks in the decades to come.

Around 1 km south of the main railway station is the Technical University complex, including the massive former District Court (Landgericht). Its cruciform east wing served during the Second World War and for some time

---

Memorial Site Münchner Platz Dresden:
Mon. – Fri. 10 am – 4 pm, Sat., Sun. 10 am – 6 pm
Tel. 0351 46331990, www.stsg.de

Brühl Palace, also known as Marcolini Palace, built in 1728 by Augustus the Strong for one of his numerous mistresses.

thereafter as a prison with around 700 cells. Some 2,000 opponents of the Nazi regime were guillotined here. After the war it was the turn of former Nazi officials, opponents of the new SED regime. The death cells have been kept in intact as a **memorial**, like the memorial on Richtplatz and the "Resistance Fighter", a bronze statue by A. Wittig.

▲ *Chapel in the Inner Catholic Cemetery in Friedrichstadt*

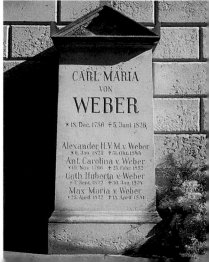

Grave of the famous ▶
opera composer
Carl Maria von Weber

CARL MARIA
VON
WEBER
★ 18. Dec. 1786 ✝ 5. Juni 1826

Alexander H. V. M. v. Weber
★ 8. Jan. 1825 ✝ 31. Okt. 1844
Ant. Carolina v. Weber
★ 19. Nov. 1796 ✝ 23. Febr. 1852
Cath. Huberta v. Weber
★ 7. Sept. 1822 ✝ 30. Jan. 1374
Max Maria v. Weber
★ 25. April 1822 ✝ 13. April 1881

One of the largest parks at the edge of the Altstadt is Blüher Park, a few hundred metres to the north of the main railway station. This marks the site of the **German Hygiene Museum** ㉘ , which was founded in 1912 at the initiative of Odol manufacturer K. A. Lingner. The reconstructed museum was opened in 1930, and underwent extensive renovations and upgrades at the hands of Prof. P. Kulka in 2002. In addition to the permanent "Abenteuer Mensch" (Adventures of mankind) exhibition with the "Gläserne Frau" (Glass woman) and the Children's Museum (Kindermuseum), it also features special interdisciplinary exhibitions on current topics.

The Bürgerwiese containing numerous sculptures is found to the south of Blüher Park, with the stadium of the well-known Dynamo Dresden football club and an open-air swimming pool to the east. Behind it, beyond Lennéstraße, we find the city's largest and most popular public park, the **Volkspark Großer Garten**. At the Northwest corner of the park, interested visitors can tour the new "see-thru" Volkswagen plant, or board the park railway to explore the vast grounds at a leisurely pace. Laid out in 1676 as a royal pheasant-run, it was converted in 1683 into a Baroque park. In the second half of the 19th century it was landscaped and a zoological and botanical garden installed. Of the numerous statues, the groups at either end of the main alley and the

Mosaic fountain by Hans Poelzig in Großer Garten (Big Garden)

Marble group "Time snatches Beauty" by Pietro Balestra in front of the Gartenpalais (Garden Palace)

The Public Park is the most popular park in Dresden. At its centre is the former Summer Palace of the Electors of Saxony on the shore of the Palace Lake.

over-sized sandstone statues at the end of the parallel Hercules Alley are particularly worth noting. The latter were designed around 1695 by B. Permoser and show scenes from the myth of Hercules.

The edifice in the centre of the Grosser Garten was erected in 1680 as a summer palace for the heir apparent and later Elector John George III, father of Augustus the Strong. It was Dresden's first Baroque

Mozart Fountain by Hermann Hosaeus in the Bürgerwiese Park

building, richly decorated with ornaments, busts, figures and cartouches. Unfortunately the palace has not yet been restored and very little can be guessed at present of its former glory, although remnants of the Baroque splendour are still to be seen in the lake and the six residential buildings.

German Hygiene Museum:
Permanent "Abenteuer Mensch" (Adventures of mankind) exhibition, "Unsere 5 Sinne" (Our 5 senses) Children's Museum, venue for meetings, lectures and concerts; Lingnerplatz 1, Tue.–Sun., public holidays 10am-6pm, tel. 0351 48460, www.dhmd.de

The Leonhardi Museum, the painter Eduard Leonhardi's former house and

studio. Exhibition of works by local young artists.

Blue Wonder and White Stag

Since 1893 a bridge about 6 km to the east of the city centre has connected the former suburbs of Blasewitz and Loschwitz, now part of the city of Dresden. Claus Köpcke designed this 150 m long iron structure which spans the Elbe without piers and which was regarded as a technical miracle at the time. As the iron elements were painted blue the bridge earned its nickname the **"Blue Wonder"** (Blaues Wunder) and became one of the most familiar landmarks of the city.

From the mid-19th century Blasewitz was an elegant residential suburb of Dresden. The Jagdhaus (hunting lodge), mentioned in 1683 as an inn, is one of the oldest buildings in the area. In the 19th century phylloxera destroyed the vineyards in Loschwitz on the other side of the river and the wine-growers sold their land to wealthy inhabitants of the city. On one side of the river are the older villas of Blasewitz; on the other side in Loschwitz magnificent houses and chateaux looking down onto the Elbe were erected – such as Villa Stockhausen or the romantic castle-like Albrechtsberg and Eckberg. In 1785 – 87 Schiller worked on his play Don Carlos in a garden house in the vineyards belonging to Gottfried Körner. One of the rooms has been furnished in the style of the period.

A cableway leads up to the former spa **Weisser Hirsch** (White Stag), around 100 m above Loschwitz. Today this part of the city is one of the most select residential areas of Dresden. From here and from Loschwitzhöhe opposite visitors are offered a very pleasant view of this part of the Elbe valley. Loschwitzhöhe is best reached by a suspension railway, the oldest of its type in the world.

The "Diesbar", one of the oldest paddle steamers in Germany, in front of the "Blue Wonder" bridge

▲ *The "Blue Wonder"*

*Cable railway to ▶
the Weißer Hirsch
(white stag)*

▼ *Suspension railway
from Körnerplatz to
Löschwitzhöhe*

Pillnitz Castle

Around 7 km upstream from Loschwitz is the pleasure palace of Pillnitz Castle. Shortly before, we pass through Hosterwitz, where Carl concerts, are held there frequently. At the level of Pillnitz Castle, a favourite excursion destination throughout the year for the people of Dresden and visitors to the city, is an elongated islet and nature re-

Carl Maria von Weber memorial in Hosterwitz. The former wine-grower house served as a summer house for the composer between 1818 and 1824. Here he composed various parts of his opera "Der Freischütz".

Maria von Weber worked on his opera Der Freischütz. The summer house of the former musical director was built in Biedermeier style around 1820. Various relics of the composer are to be found in the memorial and literary. Musical performances, including chamber serve on the Elbe, with rare flora and fauna. Opposite was a small chateau owned by the aristocratic von Bünau family, which was acquired by the ruling family in 1694. Augustus the Strong gave Pillnitz to his mistress, Countess Cosel, in 1707. When she fell from grace in

Carl-Maria von Weber memorial:
Dresdner Straße 44, Wed. – Sun. 1 pm – 6 pm,
Tel. 0351 2618234, www.museen-dresden.de

View of the Elbe and of Hosterwitz with the romantic sailors' church "Maria am Wasser"

1717 Augustus ordered the chateau to be converted into an oriental pleasure palace for land and riverside festivities. Architects Longuelune and Pöppelmann first constructed the Riverside Palace (Wasserpalais), completed in 1723, with its elegant steps going down to the Elbe. Augustus was able to sail right up to the palace in a gondola, his favourite means of transport, and alight between the two gilded sphinxes at the bottom of the steps. The roofs and mouldings clearly show the

Pillnitz castle and gardens

Chinese influence fashionable at the time. Directly opposite the Riverside Palace was the Upper Palace (Bergpalais), constructed in 1722 – 24. Towards the end of the 18th century the wings were added and around 1824, after the Countess's palace had burnt down, a Classicist linking building was erected in its place.

Pillnitz Castle not only harmoniously combines Baroque and Renaissance styles but also fits ideally into its natural setting. The magnificent centrepiece of the inner garden is the Baroque pond with its huge fountain surrounded by well-tended gardens. These give way to a topiary garden which continues in the 500 m long, 40 m wide chestnut-lined avenue. Here the courtiers used to play maille, a forerunner of golf.

The most notable of the gigantesque trees in the English Garden is a huge plane tree on the banks of the lake with a trunk more than six metres in circumference. Even more popular with visitors, especially when in bloom, is the oldest camellia in Europe, delivered from Japan in 1770. Today it is over 8 metres high and 9 metres in diameter and has been located since 1992 in a modern glass and iron greenhouse.

The inside of the sumptuous pleasure palace has also been restored and contains the Craft Museum (Museum für Kunsthandwerk) with exhibits from the 13th to 20th centuries including furniture, glass,

Pillnitz Castle: fountain in the Baroque Garden in front of the Upper Palace. The summer residence was designed by Augustus the Strong in Oriental style.

Watteau hall in the Bergpalais (Upper Palace)

ceramic, metal and textile objects such as the valuable Pirna Antependium, an artistic silk embroidery from the 14th century, the throne of Augustus the Strong, and an enormous cupboard from the court joinery.

Information

Castle Museum in the New Palace: *May to October Tue. – Sun. 10 am – 6 pm, November to April guided tours on weekends, Tel. 351 2613260*
Museum of Arts in the Bergpalais and the Wasserpalais: *May to October Tue. – Sun. 10 am – 6 pm, closed November to April, Tel. 0351 26130*
www.schlosspillnitz.de

Chinese Pavilion

Walnut cupboard

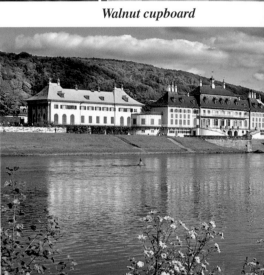

Dance-hall

Wasserpalais from the bank of

Augustus the Strong's gondola

Jug with plastic decorations

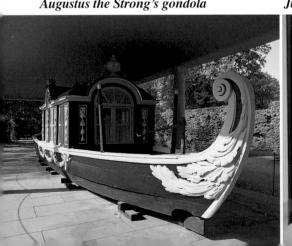

Wasserpalais (Water Palace)

the Elbe in Kleinzschachwitz

Back of a chair

Pewter ware

Wasserpalais (Water Palace)

Country church "Zum Heiligen Geist" (of the Holy Spirit)

Großsedlitz Baroque Gardens

Like Pillnitz, the **Baroque Gardens in Großsedlitz** can be reached not only by car or bus but by one of the Weisse Flotte ships. This delightful Baroque park is close to Heidenau on a hill overlooking the river. In 1719 Count von Wackerbarth bought a burnt-out manor on this site. He had the Friedrich Pavilion (Friedrichschlösschen) and Upper Orangery (Obere Orangerie) built from plans by Pöppelmann. When the property was acquired by the crown necessary funds. Although never completed, the most impressive Baroque park in Saxony was laid out here according to plans by Knöffel. Perhaps the most well conceived element is the Baroque staircase by Pöppelmann opposite the Lower Orangery with its flowing balustrades and music-playing "Silent Music" (Stille Musik) putti. The visitors who stream here every year from the bustle of Dresden appreciate the quiet surroundings and artistic stone sculptures. The summer events which take place here regularly continue a tradition

Großsedlitz Baroque Gardens with Friedrich Pavillion and Upper Orangery

in 1723, Augustus the Strong planned to build a large hilltop palace here, but was unable to summon up the initiated at the time of Augustus with the annual festival of the Polish Order of the White Eagle.

Saxon Switzerland and Königstein Fortress

One of the most popular excursions for visitors to Dresden is a trip to the Elbe sandstone massif (Elbsandsteingebirge) known as Saxon Switzerland. After 20 km by road we reach Pirna with its interesting town hall and parish church (both 16th century).

A further 10 km and we reach the car park below the imposing **Königstein Fortress** (Festung Königstein). After the medieval castle passed into the hands of the Wettins in the early 15th century, it was kept so well defended that no enemy ever dared to attack it. For this reason the owners also used it to keep their treasures (most recently after 1940) and as a refuge in times of war. It also served as a high-security jail, and in 1870/71 and both World Wars as a prisoner-of-war camp.

The hilltop, originally crowned by jagged rocks, was gradually flattened with the building of the fortress to form a 9.5 hectare plateau over which the defensive structures are spread.

Thanks to its beautiful location 230 metres above the Elbe with an outstanding view of the Elbe sandstone massif the fortress was often used by the rulers to entertain official visitors and to show them how well the country was being defended. Dignitaries who visited the fortress include Peter I Tsar of Russia, Prussian kings Frederick William I

Loop of the Elbe between Lilienstein and the southern part of Königstein fortress with Christiansburg (Christian Castle)

Bastion bridge – connection with Neurathen fortress over the ravine

and Frederick II, and the Emperor Napoleon.

Continuing a further 6 km upstream a bridge crosses the Elbe at Bad Schandau. In Rathmannsdorf we stop on the left and follow the signs to **Bastei** near Rathen, a paradise for hikers and climbing enthusiasts, but also with car parks to enable visitors to reach the vantage points without difficulty. The view over the labyrinthine gorge with its bizarrely shaped rocks is well worth the effort. The Bastei bridge, built in 1851, crosses the ravine between the rocks, giving walkers

◀ Bad
Schandau

Wehlen ▶

Stolpen ▶
Castle,
Seiger
and Cosel
Towers

◀ Hohenstein
Castle

a magnificent view of the Elbe valley and the Lilienstein and Königstein table mountains. Around 500 steps down is the Amselsee lake and an open-air theatre quarried from the rock with seats for 2,000 spectators. Originally laid out in 1938 for the Karl May festival, it is also used today to stage operas. In 1954 the Saxon State Theatre took over the theatre and have performed a number of operas there, notably Der Freischütz and Hänsel and Gretel.

An easy detour of 10 km at Lohmen on the way back to Dresden takes visitors to **Stolpen** with its medieval castle dating from 1100, made famous by Countess Cosel, erstwhile mistress of Augustus the Strong who was held captive there for more than 48 years from 1716 to 1765 after she had fallen from grace.

The best way back to Dresden is by way of Radeberg and the Dresdener Heide recreation park.

Via Radebeul to Moritzburg

On the right bank of the Elbe, leaving Dresden to the west, are the Lössnitz hills, centre of the Saxon wine-growing region. In the heart of the vineyards and gardens is **Radebeul,** hometown of the famous author Karl May (1842–1912). His onetime residence, Villa "Shatterhand", contains a collection of objects owned by him and – in the neighbouring wild west blockhouse "Villa Bear Fat" – some 850 original artefacts relating to the history and culture of the prairie Indians, one of Europe's most valuable ethnological collections.

The district of Kötzschenbroda is also well worth a visit. Situated in the Elbe flats its magnificent high street is lined with many homely inns and shady places to sit, and is considered by many as a tip for visitors to Dresden.

Just 10 km to the north of Radebeul are the Moritzburger Lakelands (Moritzburger Teichgebiet) and **Moritzburg Castle** (Schloss Moritzburg), an imposing hunting lodge built by Augustus the Strong. Lovers of nostalgia should make the journey from Radebeul-Weisses Ross by narrow-gauge railway. The Baroque structure with its four

Karl May Museum:
Karl-May-Straße 5, Radebeul, Tel. 0351 837300
March to October, Tue. – Sun. 9 am – 6 pm, November to February,
Tue. – Sun. 10 am – 4 pm, www.karl-may-museum.de

Moritzburg Castle: baroque hunting lodge built by Augustus the Strong on an artificial island near Dresden.

round towers on an artificial island can be seen from far off. It was originally the site of a hunting lodge on a rocky promontory belonging to Duke Maurice of Saxony, before Augustus's favourite architect Pöppelmann built the terraced island and castle together with an approach dike and parklands in 1723–26. The balustrade on the upper terrace is decorated by a number of vases and putti, starting with two hunters blowing hunting horns. Above the portal the initials AR (Augustus Rex) commemorate the commissioning monarch. Even in this remote castle he indulged not only his love of hunting but also his passion for collection, and had the rooms decorated with numerous paintings, porcelain vases,

and hunting trophies. The elk palms and collection of red deer antlers are particularly impressive. Included in the collection are a set of 66-point Moritzburger red stag antlers, 2.40 m wide and weighing 20 kg, the largest set of antlers in the world, coming from an animal killed in 1696 by Elector Frederick III of Brandenburg, the antlers of a 10,000-year-old giant stag presented by Tsar Peter I of Russia, and "Willkomm", a 36-point set of antlers, hollowed out and converted into a drinking vessel. Also worth looking at is the white chapel with its gilded ornamentations and the two rooms occupied by Augustus with their richly decorated leather wall hangings, paintings, valuable furniture and other objects. The gar-

dens form a magnificent setting for parties and masked balls.

The gardens and extensive forest land interspersed with ponds are ideal for leisurely walks. One route starts at the eastern end of the castle lake on the other side of the road. After a few minutes we pass the Waldschänke hotel and restaurant, built around 1770 and still retaining some of its original features. Shortly afterwards, to the left, is the **Pheasantry Pavilion** (Fasanenschlösschen – ca. 1775). The artistically curved roof topped by lanterns reflects the fashion for far-eastern style elements, even in the Rococo period. Behind the pink and green facade the few rooms, including the elector's study, are furnished with original trappings and today house an ornithological museum. The terrace and park are decorated in the style of the time with sculptures, while high vases and elaborate Leda fountains adorn the canal. The front of the pavilion with its double-flight stairway leads to the lake and miniature harbour. The painted brick wall on the lighthouse is reminiscent of structures to be found on the North Sea coast. The complex was used to stage "naval battles" for the entertainment of the monarchs. The royal gondola also docked in the harbour, as the Elector – usually with female company – sailed over to the island with its romantic little house. Early this century a dam

Moritzburg Castle: *Tel. 035207 8730, www.schloss-moritzburg.de*
Natural life park: *Tel. 03 5207 99790*
Käthe Kollwitz memorial: *Tel. 035207 82818*
www.kollwitz-moritzburg.de

Lighthouse on the lake

Romantic Pheasantry Pavilion

was built across the lake by causing the water level in the harbour to drop by 1.50 metres. Most of the ponds today are used for carp breeding.

▼ *Moritzburg Castle, Guest room*

Meißen

From the top of the Burgberg, the late Gothic Albrechtsburg castle and cathedral already greet the onlooker from afar. This ensemble is as symbolic for Meißen as its vineyards, wine taverns and its world-famous porcelain. The market square characterised by architecture from the Middle Ages, creates a particularly charming centre. Narrow lanes lead away from the centre to the historical castle in which Augustus the Strong founded the first European porcelain manufactory in 1710 – under the direction of inventor Böttger and in the strictest secrecy. On our stroll, we come across proud town houses which bear witness to the prosperity of former centuries when Meißen ranked among the most important trading places on the River Elbe alongside Hamburg and Magdeburg. After climbing the hill, we are rewarded with a breathtaking view of the old town.

View of the River Elbe across to Albrechtsburg castle and the cathedral

Tips and adresses from A to Z

Assistance for the physically disabled: Information from Tourist information, Tel. 0351 501501

Camping: Caravan camping Nord Elsterweg 13, Tel. 0351 8809792; Intercamp Mockritz, Tel. 0351 4715250; Wostra, Trieske Str. 100, Tel. 0351 2013254; outside of Dresden: Campingplatz Mittelteichbad, Boxdorf, Volkersdorf, Altfranken, Radeburg, Scharfenberg, Bad Schandau

Car rental: German Automobile Club (ADAC), Tel. 0351 2516327; Avis, Tel. 0351 4969613; Europcar, Tel. 0351 4969535, 0351 8814590,0351 5022251; Hertz, Tel. 0351 2328218, 0351 5662840; Sixt, Tel. 0351 4956012, 0351 4954105

City sightseeing tours: short bus tours (90 minutes) daily from Dr.-Külz-Ring and Augustus Bridge; 3-hour tours including Pillnitz Park daily by double-decker bus from Dr.-Külz-Ring and by tram from Postplatz/Zwinger. Streetcar tours daily from Postplatz.

Emergency assistance/Emergency services: police, Tel. 110; fire brigade, Tel. 112; emergency medical assistance, Tel. 115; urgent medical assistance (day and night), Tel. 80452251; ambulance, Tel. 19222; recorded announcements with physicians and pharmacists on call, Tel. 011500

Government agencies: Freistaat Sachsen Sächsische Staatsregierung, Archivstrasse 1, Tel. 0351 5640; State Capital of Dresden, City Administration, Dr.-Külz-Ring, Tel. 0351 4880

Information: Local transport, Dresdener Verkehrsbetriebe AG, service telephone 0351 8571011: German Rail/Deutsche Bahn AG information, Tel. 01805 996633; Air travel, airport information: 0351 8613360/62/70

Road assistance: Automobile Club ADAC, Tel. 0180 2222222

Railways: Park Railway, cableway, funicular, narrow-gauge railway (Radebeul – Moritzburg – Radeburg)

Saxony Steamship Company: Tel. 0351 866090

Special events: May: Riverboat Fleet Parade; International Dixieland Festival; Music Festival (May – June); June: Dance Festival, Elbhangfest; July: Movie nights on the banks of the Elbe; August – September: Stallions' Parade in Moritzburg; December: Striezelmarkt

Swimming baths: Indoor: Nordbad, Louisenstrasse, Tel. 0351 8032360; Georg-Arnold-Bad, Hauptallee, Tel. 0351 4942203; Erlebnisbad Elbamare, Wölfnitzer Ring, Tel. 0351 410090; Schwimmhalle Senftenberger Str., Tel. 0351 2843161; Schwimmhalle Freiberger Platz, Tel. 0351 4881690; Schwimmhalle Radebeul, Tel. 0351 8305205

Taxi: Tel. 0351 211211

Theatres:
Saxony State Opera in Dresden, Post Office Box 120712, 01067 Dresden, Tel.0351 4911-0;
Dresden Philharmonic Orchestra, Palace of Culture at the Old Market, Post Office Box 120424, 01005 Dresden, Tel. 0351 4866866;
Dresden City Theatre, Theatre at the Zwinger, Ostra-Allee 3, 01067 Dresden, Tel. 0351 4913555;
Showcase Theatre in Neustadt, Glacisstr. 28, 01099 Dresden, Tel. 0351 4313555;
City Operetta, Prinaer Landstrasse 131, 01257 Dresden, Tel. 0351 20799-0;
Theatre of the Young Generation, Meissener Landstrasse 152, 01157 Dresden, Tel. 0351 42912-0;
State Theatres of Saxony, Meissener Landstrasse 152, 01445 Radebeul, Tel. 0351 89540;
Dresden's Cabaret Theatre "Herkuleskeule", Sternplatz 1, 01067 Dresden, Tel. 0351 4925555;
Brettl Theatre Barge, Terrassenufer, 01067 Dresden, Tel. 0351 4969450;
Palace of Culture, Schlossstrasse 2, 01067 Dresden, Tel. 0351 4866-0;
Dresden Comedy Theatre, Freiberger Strasse 39, 01067 Dresden, Tel. 0351 866410;
Jazz Club "Tonne", Königstraße 15, 01099 Dresden, Tel. 0351 8026017

Tourist Information Office, Prager Str. 2b (room reservations, events, theatre tickets), service centre tel. 0351 501501; Street address: At the QF-Passage (Quartier an der Frauenkirche), Neumarkt 2, 01067 Dresden; in the main train station, Wiener Platz 4, 01069 Dresden, www.dresden.de

Vantage points: Holy Cross Church, Hausmann Tower, Church of the Epiphany, Town Hall Tower Church of our Lady

Youth hostels: Dresden Youth Hostel, Maternisstrasse 22, Tel. 0351 492620; Hübnerstr. 11, Tel. 0351 470667; Radebeul, Weintraubenstr. 12, Tel. 0351 8382880

Zoological gardens: Tel. 0351 478060 www.zoo-dresden.de

City street map legend:

① Augustus Bridge
② Royal Palace
③ Hofkirche
④ Theaterplatz
⑤ Semper Opera House
⑥ Zwinger
⑦ Taschenberg Palace and Cholera Fountain
⑧ Old Marketplace
⑨ New Town Hall
⑩ Landhaus
⑪ Albertinum
⑫ New Marketplace
⑬ Cosel Palace
⑭ Church of Our Lady
⑮ Procession of Princes
⑯ Brühl Terrace
⑰ Synagogue
⑱ Maurice Monument
⑲ Goldener Reiter
⑳ Church of the Epiphany
㉑ Albertplatz
㉒ Art Passage
㉓ Pfund's Dairy
㉔ Japanische Palais
㉕ Jägerhof
㉖ Yenidze
㉗ Inner Catholic Cemetery
㉘ German Hygiene Museum

Key to the symbols

ℹ	Touristinformation / tourist information / informations toristiques
🏛	Museum / museum / musée
🏛	Denkmal / monument / monument
▮	Gedenkstein oder -tafel / commemorative stone or plaque / pierre commémorative, plaque commémorative
⚓ ⊙	Brunnen / well / puits
▣ ▣	Stadtrundfahrt; Stadtführung / city sightseeing tour; city walking tour / tour de ville; circuit de la ville à pied
🎭	Theater und Spielstätten / theatre / théâtre
◼ ◮	Hotel; Jugendherberge / hotel; youth hostel / hôtel; auberge de jeunesse
●—	Straßenbahnlinie mit Haltestelle / tram route with stop / ligne de tramway avec arrêt
▲—	Buslinie mit Haltest. in nur eine Fahrtrichtung / bus route with stop for travel in one direction only / arrêt d'autobus en direction unique
DB	Fernbahnhof der Deutschen Bahn AG / long-distance train station / gare principale
Ⓢ	S-Bahnhof / suburban train station / station de RER
TAXI	Taxistand / taxi rank / station de taxi
WC	öffentliche Toilette / public toilet / toilettes publiques
WC ♿	behindertengerechte öffentliche Toilette / public toilet for the disabled / toilettes publiques pour handicapés
☀	Aussichtspunkt / lookout point / point de vue panoramique
T	Dampferanlegestelle / landing stage / embarcadère
= =	Unterführung, Durchgang / subway, passageway / passage souterrain, passage
⊟	Treppe / steps / escaliers